D0558745

First
Worst
Joke Book

Dumb Jokes for Kids

By Steve Burt

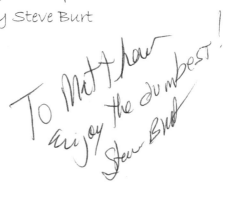

To Matthew
enjoy the dumbest!
Steve Burt

First Worst Joke Book

Dumb Jokes for Kids

By Steve Burt

ISBN-13: 978-1523356836
ISBN-10: 1523356839

Steven E. Burt
The Villages, FL 32162
352 391-8293

Dumb Jokes for Kids

For my grandkids,
Gracie and Ben,
who love dumb jokes.

1. Why do bikes fall over?
They're two-tired.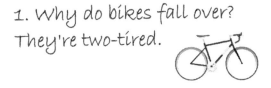

2. How does an ocean say hi?
It waves.

3. What does a boxer drink?
Punch.

4. What's a tree's favorite
drink?
Root beer.

Dumb Jokes for Kids

5. Why does the Mississippi River see so well?
It has four eyes.

6. What kind of bagel can fly?
A plain bagel.

7. Why did the can crusher quit his job?
It was soda pressing.

8. How does a train eat?
Choo choo.

9. Why can't you hear a
pterodactyl going
to the bathroom?
The "P" is silent.

10. How'd Luke Skywalker
know what Darth Vader got
him for Christmas?
He felt his presents.

11. What kind of horses roam
after the sun goes down?
Nightmares.

12. Why are ghosts such bad liars?
You can see right through them.

13. What's the best time to go to the dentist?
Tooth-hurty.

14. What's a witch's favorite subject?
Spelling.

ABC

15. Why couldn't the pirate play poker?

He was standing on the deck.

16. Why are bakers rich?
They're always making lots of dough.

17. What streets do ghosts haunt?
Dead ends.

18. What do you call cheese that doesn't belong to you?
Nacho cheese.

19. What has a
face and hands
but no body?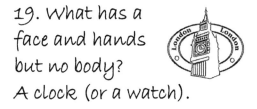
A clock (or a watch).

20. What word becomes
shorter when you add two
letters to it?
Short.

21. If the clerk at the deli
counter is five feet ten inches
tall and wears size 13 shoes,
what does he weigh?
Meat.

22. How much dirt is there in a hole that measures two feet wide by three feet long by four feet deep?
None.

23. In California you cannot take a picture of a man with a wooden leg. Why not?
You need a camera.

24. What happens when a frog's car breaks down?
It gets toad away.

25. Heard the one about the roof?
Never mind, it's over your head.

26. What do firefighters put in their soup?
Fire crackers.

27. What do sea monsters eat?
Fish and ships.

28. What bird can lift the most?
A crane.

29. What time do twins wake up?
Two.

30. What time does a shark wake up?
Eight (ate).

31. Why did the teddy bear skip breakfast?
He was already stuffed.

32. What kind of rocks are never found in the ocean? Dry ones.

33. How do you make a handkerchief dance? Put a little boogie in it.

34. Why did the chicken cross the playground? To get to the other slide.

35. What do you call a pig that knows karate? A pork chop!

36. Why do bees have
sticky hair?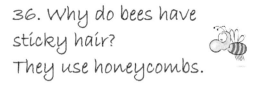
They use honeycombs.

37. Why was the man
running around his bed?
He wanted to catch up on his
sleep.

38. Why is 6 afraid of 7?
Because 7 8 9.

39. What's black
and white, black
and white, black
and white?
A penguin rolling downhill!

40. Why do cows wear bells?
Their horns don't work!

41. What does a snail say
when it's riding on a turtle's
back?
Wheeeee!

42. How did the barber win
the race?
He knew a short
cut.

43. What do you call a fake
noodle?
An impasta.

44. What do you call an
alligator in a vest?
An In-vest-i-gator.

 45. What's the
difference between
a guitar and a
fish?
You can't tuna fish.

46. Did you hear about the
race between the lettuce and
the tomato?
The lettuce was a "head," the
tomato wanted to "ketchup."

47. What do you get from a
pampered cow?
Spoiled milk.

48. What do attorneys wear
to court?
Lawsuits!

49. What gets wetter the
more it dries?
A towel.

50. What did one pencil say
to the other?
You're looking pretty
sharp.

51. What did
Bacon say to
Tomato?
Lettuce get together.

52. What is the hardest
working part of your eye?
The pupil.

53. Why did the picture go to
jail?
It was framed.

54. What do you get when
you cross a fish with an
elephant?
Swimming trunks.

55. What do you call a baby monkey?
A chimp off the old block.

56. Who earns a living driving their customers away?
A taxi driver (or a bus driver).

57. How do you shoot a killer bee?
With a BB gun.

58. What happened when the dog swallowed a firefly?
It barked with de-light.

59. What stays in the corner but travels all over the world?
A postage stamp.

60. Why did the computer go to the doctor?
It had a virus.

61. What do you get when you cross a cow and a duck?
Milk and quackers.

62. What do you call a
sleeping bull?
A bulldozer.

 63. What is the
tallest building in
the world?
The library, because it has the
most stories.

64. What do you call a belt
with a watch on it?
A waist of time.

65. Why is England the
wettest country?
Because the queen has
reigned over it for 50+ years.

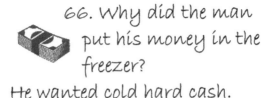 66. Why did the man put his money in the freezer?

He wanted cold hard cash.

67. What do you get when you cross a snowman with a vampire?
Frostbite.

68. What is the best day to go to the beach?
On a Sunday.

69. What bow can't be tied?
A rainbow!

70. What season is it when you are on a trampoline?
Spring time.

71. Where do computers go when they want to dance?
A disc-o.

72. What has one head, one foot, and four legs?
A bed.

73. What's the difference between a teacher and a train?
The teacher says spit your gum out but the train says choo-choo-choo.

74. Why did the bird go to the hospital?
For a tweetment.

75. What sound do porcupines make when they kiss?
Ouch.

76. Why did the guy look for fast food on his friend? Because his friend said, "Dinner's on me."

77. What's brown and has a head and a tail but no legs? A penny.

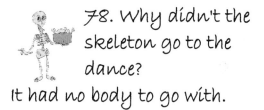

78. Why didn't the skeleton go to the dance? It had no body to go with.

79. Why are pirates called pirates?
Because they arrrrr.

80. What do prisoners use to call each other?
Cell phones.

81. Where do snowmen keep their money?
In the snowbank.

82. What washes up on very small beaches?
Microwaves.

83. What runs through towns, over hills, and across deserts, but doesn't move?
The road.

84. Why did thunder and lightning suddenly appear in the lab?
The scientists were brainstorming.

85. Why did the peach go out with a prune?
It couldn't find a date.

86. Why did the traffic light turn red?
It had to change in front of everybody.

87. What never asks questions but gets plenty of answers?
A phone.

88. What makes an octopus giggle?
Ten-tickles.

 89. Why can't a
human being's nose
be 12 inches long?
Because then it
would be a foot.

90. What has four wheels and
flies?
A garbage truck.

91. What starts with a P,
ends with an E, and has over
1000 letters in it?
Post Office.

92. What did the blanket say
to the bed?
Don't worry, I've
got you covered.

93. How many
books can you
put in an empty
backpack?
One. Then it's no longer
EMPTY.

94. What kind of flooring do
they use in daycare centers?
Infant-tile.

95. What kind of button
won't unbutton?
A bellybutton.

96. What did the triangle
say to the circle?
I don't see your
point.

97. Why do sea-gulls fly
over the sea?
Because if they flew over the
bay, they'd be bagels!

98. What dog keeps
the best time?
A watch dog.

99. What did the
man say to the wall?
One more crack out
of you and I'll plaster you.

100. Why did the tomato
turn red?
It saw the salad dressing.

101. What sound did the
grape make when it got
stepped on?
It let out a little wine.

102. What did the judge say
when the skunk walked into
the court room?
Odor in the court.

103. Why do skeletons refuse to fight each other? They don't have the guts.

104. What did the janitor yell when he suddenly jumped out of the closet? Supplies!

105. Why was the kid's report card wet?

It was below C level.

106. Why did the robber take a bath?
So he could have a clean getaway.

107. What music scares balloons?
Pop music.

108. Why did the boy tiptoe past the medicine cabinet?
He didn't want to wake the sleeping pills.

109. What goes up when the
rain comes down?
An umbrella.

110. Why did the belt get
sent to prison?
Someone saw it holding up a
pair of pants.

111. What did the stamp say
to the envelope?
Stick with me,
we'll go places.

112. What kind of lights did Noah use on the Ark?
Flood lights.

113. Which month do soldiers hate?
March.

114. Why do golfers wear two pairs of pants?
In case they get a hole in one.

115. Why would someone throw a clock out the window?
To see time fly.

116. When do you stop at green and go at red?
When you're eating a watermelon.

117. How did the farmer mend his pants?
With cabbage patches.

118. What do you use to repair a broken tomato?
Tomato Paste.

119. Why did the baby strawberry cry?
Because he heard his parents were in a jam.

120. What did the
hamburger name his
daughter?
Patty.

121. What kind of eggs do
bad chickens lay?
Deviled eggs.

 122. What key
opens the door on
Thanksgiving?
Tur-key.

123. Why did the cookie go to
the hospital?
It felt crummy.

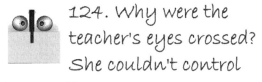 124. Why were the teacher's eyes crossed? She couldn't control her pupils.

125. What do you call a bear with no socks on?
Bare-foot.

126. What can you serve but never eat?
A volleyball (or a ping pong ball or a shuttlecock).

127. What kind of shoes do spies wear?
Sneakers.

128. Why did the soccer player bring string to the game?
In case he needed to tie the score.

129. Why is a baseball team like a muffin?
Both need a good batter.

130. Why do watermelons have weddings?
Because they cantaloupe.

131. How do baseball players stay cool?
They sit in front of their fans.

132. Why was the math book sad?
It had a lot of problems to work out.

133. What runs all day and night but doesn't get anywhere?
Your refrigerator.

134. What is an astronaut's favorite place on the computer keyboard?
The space bar.

135. Why is basketball such a messy sport?
The players are always dribbling on the floor.

136. How do you communicate with a fish?
Drop him a line.

137. Where do sheep go for haircuts?
To the Baa Baa shop.

138. What does a shark like to eat with peanut butter?
A little jellyfish.

139. What cereal do cats like for breakfast?
Mice Crispies!

140. Why is it impossible for a leopard to hide?
It's always spotted.

141. What do you get when you cross a cat with a lemon?
A sour puss!

142. Why do birds fly south for the winter?
It's easier than walking.

143. Why does a hummingbird hum?
It doesn't know the words.

144. What goes up and down but doesn't move?
The temperature.

145. Which weighs more—a ton feathers or a ton of bricks?
Neither, they both weigh a ton.

146. What runs but can't walk?
A faucet.

147. What's always taken before you get it?
Your picture.

148. Why did the tree go to the dentist?
To get a root canal.

149. What did the nose say to the finger?
Stop picking on me.

150. What did the necktie say to the hat?
You go on ahead and I'll hang around.

 151. What did one plate say to the other?
Dinner's on me.

152. Why did the girl bring lipstick and eye shadow to school?
She had a make-up exam.

153. What did one eyeball say to the other eyeball?
Just between you and me, something smells.

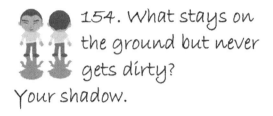 154. What stays on the ground but never gets dirty?
Your shadow.

155. What's the difference between a cat and a frog?
A cat has nine lives but a frog croaks every night.

156. Why can you never trust atoms?
They make up everything.

157. Did you hear the one about the weirdo who said No?
???

158 Where does Batman go when he has to pee?
To the Batroom.

First Worst Joke Book

If you enjoyed Steve Burt's First Worst Joke Book, you'll no doubt also love his Second Worst Joke Book. They're both part of his Dumb Jokes for Kids series. Available in print or Kindle e-book.

Steve Burt writes lots of other good stuff, too. There's the FreeKs series, featuring paranormal teen detectives, winner of 4 Mom's Choice Awards. He's also got ghost story collections (Stories to Chill the Heart series), which are for young adults and have won the Bram Stoker Award and the New England Book Festival Award. They can be found on Amazon or at the author's website.

www.SteveBurtBooks.com

45850876R00030

Made in the USA
San Bernardino, CA
19 February 2017